THE STOCK MARKET CRASH, 1929

In September, 1929, America was enjoying the unprecedented prosperity of the Jazz Age. Gambling freely on the stock market in hopes of making a quick fortune, many people did not anticipate trouble. Suddenly, and seemingly without warning, stock prices started to fall. Then, with gathering momentum, values tumbled. Fear set in over the land and men panicked as stocks depreciated day after day. Finally, on Black Tuesday, October 29, 1929, an infamous day in American history, an orgy of selling brought the greatest collapse of the stock market. This crash ended the era of good times and started an economic slowdown that resulted in the great depression of the nineteen-thirties.

☆ ☆ ☆

PRINCIPALS

JOHN J. RASKOB, Democratic National Chairman, who said that everybody ought to be rich.

HERBERT C. HOOVER, President of the United States, who took little action on the stock crisis until it was too late.

ROGER BABSON, economic writer, who predicted the great stock crash.

IRVING FISHER, optimistic economics professor, who believed that stock prices would remain steady.

CHARLES E. MITCHELL, head of the National City Bank, who did not worry about the crash at first.

ALBERT H. WIGGIN, chairman of the Chase National Bank

WILLIAM C. POTTER, president of the Guaranty Trust Company

SEWARD PROSSER, chairman of the Bankers Trust Company

THOMAS W. LAMONT, senior partner at J. P. Morgan

} Men who represented banks in supporting stock prices

RICHARD WHITNEY, president of the New York Stock Exchange, who placed first bids to support stock prices.

ARTHUR CUTTEN, WILLIAM C. DURANT, JESSE LIVERMORE, FISHER BROTHERS, VAN SWERINGEN BROTHERS, MICHAEL J. MEEHAN, IVAR KREUGER, speculators who manipulated the values of stock.

Panicky crowds milling in Wall Street at the height of the crash. (Brown Brothers)

A FOCUS BOOK ⬦➤

The Stock Market Crash, 1929

Panic on Wall Street Ends the Jazz Age

by Ray and Roselyn Hiebert

FRANKLIN WATTS, INC.

575 Lexington Avenue   New York, N.Y. 10022

For Bella Peyser
Who lost on October 29, 1929
But gained on November 5, 1929

SBN: 531-01015-5
Library of Congress Catalog Card Number: 73-115411
Copyright © 1970 by Franklin Watts, Inc.
Printed in the United States of America
3   4   5

Contents

*The New York Stock Exchange and a view up Wall Street in the 1920's.
(Brown Brothers)*

Tuesday, September 3

FINDS PROSPERITY WIDE
Credit Men's Association Holds Basic Strength Makes Serious Reverses Unlikely

Wall Street Journal, September 4, 1929

Weather made front-page headlines in the New York daily papers on the sweltering Tuesday of September 3, 1929. The day before, a record-breaking 92-degree heat wave had sent people scrambling to the beaches for the Labor Day holiday. More than 900,000 sunbathers had invaded Coney Island and then had jammed rail terminals and tunnels coming back into the city. Automobiles trying to get through the Holland Tunnel were backed up for five miles.

This particular Tuesday marked a final moment in a decade of enthusiastic stock market speculation. On this day, stock prices soared to their all-time high for that period. Yet the news of such prosperity was so commonplace that it was buried in the financial pages of newspapers.

Despite prosperity, however, between that heat-filled day of September 3 and a dismal day in November two months later, many Americans watched their fortunes vanish. Their hopes of joining the growing ranks of new millionaires turned into nightmares of despair. Within that brief two-month time span, the optimism of the affluent Jazz Age of the 1920's faded away and was replaced by doubt, uncertainty, and finally the poverty of the Great Depression of the 1930's.

[1]

But on Tuesday, September 3, 1929, few anticipated such disaster. Mankind seemed to be making great progress. A world war that was supposed to end all wars had been fought. Women had won the right to vote. New machines were making life easier. Gasoline automobiles had brought swift mobility to the average American. Wireless radio had brought instant music and information into the home, and moving pictures were entertaining millions.

The years between 1920 and 1929 were given many names. They were called the Roaring Twenties, the Dry Decade, the New Era, the Age of Business, the Lost Generation, and the Jazz Age. The last summed up the era as well as any. It was a time of loud and carefree music of popular dance bands. Nearly everyone listened to jazz phonograph records on victrolas and went to the new talking pictures to see Al Jolson in *The Jazz Singer*.

The 1920's were also years of revolution in manners and morals. Puritanical and Victorian ideals were swept aside as women wore their skirts daringly above their knees and bobbed their hair to shocking lengths. They painted their faces with rouge and lipstick and smoked once-forbidden cigarettes.

Gay and sophisticated flappers danced the Charleston into the wee hours of the morning at the local speakeasy, a place where illegal liquor could be purchased. An amendment to the Constitution, passed by a more sober nation immediately after the world war, had banned the sale of alcoholic beverages. This "prohibition" had led to illegal or bootlegged liquor, often made in bathtub stills and sold by bootleggers and gangsters in local speakeasies. This underworld itself became a part of American culture.

It was a new era in finance, too. Anyone could gain the new enjoyments of life through the easy installment plan, with a few dollars down and monthly payments. High-pressure advertising urged people to buy vacuum cleaners, electric iceboxes, and land in Florida. And it urged them to buy stock in the stock market, where presumably anyone could get rich quick with a few dollars on speculation. Few considered it for what it was — reckless gambling.

On September 3, 1929, stockbrokers gathered on Wall Street, as they had for more than 150 years. This street at the heart of the nation's financial district had been named for an original wall of wood built by Peter Stuyvesant in 1753 to replace a picket fence that had kept hogs and goats from straying. Wall Street ran through lower Manhattan between Trinity Church and the East River.

During colonial days a stock exchange for buying and selling stocks and bonds had been created by a group of traders. They had met under a buttonwood tree in front of 68–70 Wall Street and had signed an agreement at Corre's Hotel on March 21, 1792.

Since that time the New York Stock Exchange has grown to be the largest exchange in America and has taken a central position in financial affairs. Together with the smaller American Stock Exchange, seventeen other regional exchanges, and the over-the-counter market and commodities exchanges, this institution carries out the selling and trading of stocks and bonds for American business and industry.

In the 1920's, perhaps for the first time in American history, the stock market became a central part of everyday American life. Nearly everyone talked about stocks and bonds.

A stock is a part or a share of a business. When a person buys a stock, he owns a share in that business and has a right to help decide on its management. He receives a piece of printed paper called a stock certificate to prove his ownership. It is the price of this stock certificate that goes up and down when it and other shares of the company are bought and sold on the stock market.

A bond is a monetary loan to a company. When a person buys a

Stockbrokers' offices as they looked in the 1920's. In small board room below, a customer's man is taking an order over the telephone. (Brown Brothers)

bond and receives a bond certificate, this proves that he has loaned money to the company. Although he does not own a share in the business and has no control over its management, he receives a small additional amount of money, called interest, from the company which borrows his money. At the end of a certain period of time, the company pays back the loan and extra money in interest.

Inside the New York Stock Exchange on September 3, 1929, trading went on in one of the nation's largest rooms, five stories high. It had been opened in 1903, and an adjoining room for additional trading, called the "garage," had been added in 1922. Around the floor were eighteen horseshoe-shaped trading posts, twelve in the main room and six in the overflow room. About seventy-five stocks were traded at each post.

The broker who held a "seat" on the exchange had a membership, or the right to do business on the floor. He wore a white oval badge with a number to identify him and was entitled to appear on the floor. It was the broker who actually stood at a post and shouted his order to buy or sell stock in competition with other brokers. This activity was known as the auction.

Lining the walls of the vast room were about 1,800 telephones and 75 Teletype machines where clerks took orders to buy and sell. Information concerning each sale was sent off the floor in a pneumatic tube to a room on the fifth floor, and the news of the transaction appeared less than two minutes later on stock tickers across the country. The ticker tape was a long, narrow, single strip of paper which listed financial information. Even as early as the 1920's the prices of stocks were printed across it as well as projected on screens hanging on walls of boardrooms in all major cities.

On that hot day of September 3, 1929, at the New York Stock Exchange, 4,438,910 shares were traded, about average for that time.

[5]

All in all, Wall Street seemed quiet. Along the seven-block avenue of finance, there was little premonition of disaster.

For almost a decade since 1921, stock prices had risen in a long, sweeping, upward pattern, with a sharper upward spiral starting just two years before, in March, 1927. Since that time, prices had climbed upward with only temporary declines, until by summer of 1929 they were at the highest point in history.

It was common gossip that year that many people had become millionaires overnight through their clever stock transactions. Everyone seemed infected with the urge to make quick money. This obsession with stock speculation which had seized the nation caused quick mergers between companies. Investment trusts were created for the easy sale of new stocks. Chain stores emerged to attract investments. Business allowed all sorts of promoters and questionable tactics to create new companies for investment, and corporations loaned money easily at high interest rates to enable gambling on the stocks of all these enterprises.

"Everybody ought to be rich," proclaimed Democratic National Chairman John J. Raskob in the *Ladies Home Journal*. Many people agreed with him. During that summer of 1929 over a million people held stock "on margin." In boardrooms across America people followed the rising prices of the favorites: "Big Steel" (U.S. Steel), "Radio" (Radio Corporation of America), or "Motors" (General Motors). They carefully studied the blackboards listing current stocks and watched the ticker tapes ticking away their seemingly never-ending story of rising prices.

The stock market rivaled baseball and Mah-Jongg as the great game of the twenties. Beauty operators, bus drivers, bakers, and plumbers joined lawyers, teachers, and doctors in following financial news and buying stocks on speculation. News of the market had become available everywhere — from brokerage houses, forecasting services, and tipster sheets, as well as newspapers and radio. By late 1929 even ocean liners traveling across the Atlantic carried stock Teletype machines.

It seemed so simple and safe to buy stocks on margin that even dignified elderly ladies engaged in such speculative ventures. One had only to call a broker and tell him what to buy. Of course, cash could be paid, but it was just as easy and would stretch an investment much further to pay only a small part of the stock's total value in cash, borrowing the remainder from the broker. This was called buying on margin, and the ease of this service encouraged more people to buy more stock on credit than they could afford. As long as prices rose, this sort of speculation was safe. But if prices fell, the broker would have to send out a call for "more margin." This means the customer had to pay more cash to cover the loan for the stock purchased. If the money was not paid, the stock had to be sold for whatever it was worth at the moment on the market.

In this new era of easy investing in stock, only a few lonely voices expressed apprehension. One respected banker, Paul Warburg, warned that if the unrestrained speculation was not brought to a halt, there would be a disastrous collapse and a general depression. But most experts failed to consider that industry had slowed down after a long period of overproduction. They were not concerned that management had maintained high prices and skimmed off profits while refusing to give laborers and farmers a greater share in the rising prosperity. These profits went right back into speculation rather than salaries. Workers often did not have enough cash to purchase the overproduced goods, which piled up in the stores.

But in that halcyon fall of 1929, few took heed of these warnings. Almost everyone believed that stock prices would continue to rise.

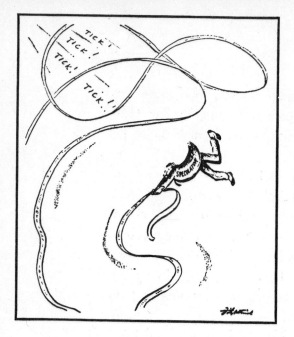

This 1929 cartoon was drawn by D. Fitzpatrick for the St. Louis Post-Dispatch *depicting a speculator's nightmare.*

President Herbert Hoover, in his presidential campaign just a year earlier, had promised "a chicken in every pot and two cars in every garage." Everyone wanted to believe him. And the unrestrained boom in stock-buying went on.

As on every working day, people on September 4, 1929, opened *The New York Times* to the financial section. They found a complete list of transactions on the stock exchange for the previous day, September 3. It was not difficult to read the stock quotations. Then as now, stocks were quoted in points; in common stock, each point stood for one dollar. Therefore, 101 was $101, 39½ was $39.50, and a stock listed at 25⅛ was valued at $25.12½, since each fraction of a point stood for 12½ cents. Four prices were usually listed in the tables. "High" was the highest price at which the stock sold during the trading session. "Low" was the lowest price for the day. "Last" was the final sale made during the trading day. But it was "net change" that was the most important.

"Net change" was the difference between the closing price of a stock for the day and the close of the last session in which it was sold. Usually, this was a twenty-four-hour change, but in less active stocks it might have meant a change of several days or weeks. The direction of the change was shown by plus or minus signs. For instance, −1 meant that today's closing price was $1.00 less than yesterday's. Readers consulting the September 3, 1929, stock quotations in *The New York Times* found the following prices for some typical stocks:

	HIGH	LOW	LAST	NET CHANGE
Allied Chemical	354½	348	354	+4
American & Foreign Power	164¾	160	160⅛	−4⅜
American Telephone & Telegraph	304	298	302½	+3⅞
Auburn Auto	498	496	497	−3
General Electric	396¼	390	391	−4½
International Telephone & Telegraph	149¼	146⅛	147⅛	+1⅛
Montgomery Ward	137⅞	134⅛	134⅛	−2⅝
Radio Corporation of America	101	98	98⅛	−1⅞
United States Steel	261¾	257⅛	257⅝	+1½

Monday, October 21

Many Stocks Set Lows on Heavy Sales

New York *Herald Tribune*, October 22, 1929

After September 3, when the all-time high in prices had been reached, Wall Street headed into the autumn financial season in an optimistic frame of mind. Soon after that, a wave of urgent selling on the afternoon of September 5 surprised brokers with its violence. Stock prices started to drop sharply.

One economic expert took heed of this unexpected tumble. Roger Babson of the New York *Herald Tribune* immediately warned his readers that a great crash was coming. Leading stocks would plummet 60 to 80 points, he predicted. But other financial prophets took little notice of the selling wave. They called the drop merely a readjustment of prices, or what they termed a "technical correction." Confident speculators seemed to agree with the experts and purchased more stocks at lower prices.

Dr. Harry Emerson Fosdick, noted pastor of the Riverside Church, was one who criticized this get-rich-quick goal of many Americans. In his Sunday sermon on October 21, Fosdick spoke out against the "money-mad generation" and the "dollar-mindedness" of the American people. "We rate things in dollars," he said. "Human life itself seems to be valued by how much we can accumulate." Other warnings of impending trouble had already appeared that summer, but they had not been widely recognized. Contracts for building had declined, and construction of houses had slowed down. Business inventories started to pile up as consumers began to spend less money. When industrial production had dropped in July, a decline in employment followed.

That fall another economic situation also led to trouble. An unhealthy foreign balance of trade resulted in foreign countries' buying more than they sold to the United States. They then had to borrow money to repay the balance. But unstable political conditions often led a foreign government to default and refuse to repay the loan. Peru was one country that had borrowed $90 million from the National City Company and would not repay the loan after the country's president, who had borrowed the money, was removed from office.

Few economists seemed to be concerned about these warning signs. Even with the sudden fall of stock prices on September 5, optimism prevailed for a quick recovery. People believed Charles E. Mitchell, influential head of the National City Bank. "There is nothing to worry about in the financial situation in the United States," he said on September 20. With that, he headed off for a European vacation.

Throughout the month of September, prices were intermittently strong and weak, falling, then rallying, only to tumble once more. By the end of September, stocks had dropped to their low mark for the year. "Unless we are to have a panic — which no one seriously believes — stocks have hit bottom," predicted R. W. McNeel, head of McNeel's Financial Service in Boston. The consensus was that McNeel's view was right, for the country was too rich and business too big to be very concerned over recent stock market rumblings. Despite the obviously downward trend of stock values, confidence remained strong

Charles E. Mitchell (right), head of the National City Bank, who believed that there was "nothing to worry about" concerning the U.S. financial situation. (Brown Brothers)

in a continuing "bull market." In a bull market, prices are generally rising; in a "bear market," prices are generally falling.

Two events were also causing increased worry. In London the collapse of an important corporate empire turned into a major stock scandal. Clarence Hatry, the corporation's prominent promoter, turned out to be a swindler and forger of certificates. Wall Street reacted with a spasm of uneasiness as money was suddenly called back to London. And in early October another bit of unexpected bad news jolted the market. The Massachusetts Department of Public Utilities refused to grant the Boston Edison Electrical Illuminating Company permission to split its stock four ways and change its par value.

The par value of a stock is the exact value that a company places on a stock certificate. If a stock is doing very well and its price has risen very high, the company may decide to split the stock. They may

[12]

divide the stock two for one, which means that the owner of one hundred shares of stocks gets another hundred shares. When the stock split takes place, it is considered a new issue of stock, and the value of the stock is divided in half. If it cost $200 before the stock split, it now costs $100. At the new lower price the stock is usually easier to sell, its price rises more rapidly, and the owner has twice as much stock to sell as before. The action of the Public Utilities Department on the Boston Edison stock implied that the value of the stock was overinflated. People who owned Boston Edison suddenly feared they would not get their money's worth out of it. Tremors shook public utility stock trading as Boston Edison fell one hundred points.

A few more operators now began to believe the current price decline was of major significance. They watched nervously as prices continued to fall, then stabilize, then drop once again. For the first time confidence of some promoters and speculators began to waver as reversals in prices were not followed by rallies. In early October the respected American Bankers Association took a nervous look at what was happening on Wall Street. They then turned to the Federal Reserve Board and asked it to investigate the entire matter of brokers' loans to speculators. They warned of great danger involved in the massive use of easy credit for stock speculation.

The Federal Reserve Board, then as now, was the economic policy-making body of the government. It guided the credit policy of the economy by setting interest rates of its twelve regional Federal Reserve banks and by selling government securities on the open market. At this critical moment in history, the Federal Reserve Board could either encourage or discourage the extension of credit by raising or lowering the rate of interest. This rate of interest was called the rediscount rate, paid by commercial banks borrowing money from a Federal Reserve bank.

All through the 1920's the Federal Reserve Board had made bank credit liberally available by loaning money at a low rediscount rate. This encouraged commercial banks to borrow from Federal Reserve banks in order to support speculative buying of stocks on credit. The banks then loaned money to brokers, and brokers in turn loaned money to customers, who bought stocks on margin. These speculators made a profit on rising stock prices and spent the gains on goods and services. Many businesses raised capital through the sale of new securities to these speculators, and thus money circulated in an increasing wave of inflation.

The Federal Reserve Board had watched this rising boom in the economy. But it had refused to raise the rediscount rate to 6 percent. This action would have slowed down the boom by making it harder to borrow money. Some bankers argued that such a raise would bring on deflation, thus slowing down the economy too much and leading to a depression. So the argument before the FRB continued unsettled. In February, 1929, the Federal Reserve Board had taken the precautionary measure of sending out letters to its member banks. The letters warned banks not to make loans for purposes of speculation. In August, 1929, the Board finally acted to raise the rediscount rate, but it chose to take no stronger or more direct action to curb speculation or to control the big boom while there was still time.

By the weekend of October 19, confusion, doubt, and uncertainty had mounted on Wall Street. Stock prices had continued to fall. Brokers started to send out telegrams asking for more margin, more money to cover falling prices. Increasing numbers of speculators began to feel the squeeze of falling prices, for many had no extra funds to fall back on. They had to draw on savings accounts to cover these unexpected margin demands from their brokers.

In Chicago, gangsters who had been heavy speculators received margin calls. Some left their brokers' offices muttering dire threats. Shortly thereafter, unidentified assailants threw dynamite into the home of one broker and hurled stench bombs into three brokerage firms. Other speculators decided on a different course of action. They had hesitated long enough. When the weekend was over and the market opened, they would sell their stocks and get out while there was still time.

On Monday, October 21, the morning gong sounded as usual at 10 A.M. From the visitors' gallery one could look down on the nervous milling and churning of brokers on the stock exchange floor as they prepared for the unusual flurry of activity they expected that morning.

There were 1,375 members of the New York Stock Exchange at that time, 25 percent more members than at the start of the year. Owning a seat on the stock exchange was a highly profitable occupation, and the purchase price of a seat had risen to record figures. That year one seat sold for as much as $625,000. Fewer than 25 years before, a seat on the stock exchange had been bought for less than $20,000. A broker received a commission on every purchase of stock, and many young men who had started at the bottom had earned great wealth from these commissions. The average yearly earnings of a broker on the exchange in 1928 was said to be $367,000, which did not include what he might make speculating in stock for himself. On an ordinary day 700 or 800 brokers, as well as the many clerks and pages necessary to the operation, would be on hand at the opening gong to do business for their accounts. But this Monday in October proved to be no ordinary day.

Just moments after the clang of the morning gong, prices began to topple in a wave of selling. As the morning passed, speculators in other cities anxiously joined in the swift sale of their stock. The volume on the floor was so great that tickers fell way behind in recording sales. As the information process slowed down and as the selling mounted hour by hour, the ticker tapes fell further behind. This left investors uncertain and confused about prices. One could easily lose his profits before finding out the actual price of his stock. This knowledge brought increased fear and apprehension. The further behind the ticker lagged, the greater became the tension. Many panicky speculators decided to sell out before prices dropped even more. Others received urgent telegrams from their brokers seeking more margin, forcing them to sell their stock against their wishes.

It was not until an hour and forty minutes after the market's close at 3:00 P.M. that the last transaction was listed on the ticker. It recorded that 6,091,870 shares had been traded, the third highest volume in history to that time. Shocked and incredulous speculators studied the losses in prices. They were somewhat consoled by one small piece of news. Just before day's end, prices had rallied and had started moving upward again. That night, brokers worked overtime to wade through the necessary paper work before the next day's sales would begin. They had to record transactions and notify some customers of margin demands. The lights burned on Wall Street through the night.

In the morning speculators picked up their newspapers apprehensively, but felt somewhat more cheerful when they turned to the financial pages. Professor Irving Fisher, a highly respected economist from Yale University, called the wave of selling a "shaking out of the lunatic fringe." Getting rid of these speculators would promote stability, he believed. For a while on Tuesday, October 22, this optimistic prediction seemed to be coming true. During the morning, prices continued the recovery which had started the last hour of the day before — then prices suddenly dropped once again.

The expected recovery in stock values had not happened. It seemed increasingly clear to speculators that the great bull market, which some had believed would continue forever, was faltering. The big question everyone tried to resolve that Tuesday night was whether prices would recover the next day or collapse completely.

By the third week in October prices had fallen an average of fifty points below their high of a few short weeks before. This can be easily seen when comparing the prices of October 21 with those for September 3.

	HIGH	LOW	LAST	NET CHANGE
Allied Chemical	323	301¼	301½	−15½
American & Foreign Power	170⅞	130½	131½	−39½
American Telephone & Telegraph	303¾	280¼	281¾	−20
Auburn Auto	440	375	375	−53
General Electric	373	338	339¼	−33¼
International Telephone & Telegraph	132¾	116	117	−13⅜
Montgomery Ward	111⅝	89¼	89¼	−22½
Radio	94¼	82¾	83	− 8½
U.S. Steel	233¼	208	209	−21¾

Wednesday, October 23

PRICES OF STOCKS CRASH IN HEAVY LIQUIDATION, TOTAL DROP OF BILLIONS

New York Times, October 24, 1929

Wednesday, October 23, was the first day that stocks really began to crash. From that day on, prices on the stock market dropped steadily.

Using the Dow-Jones stock averages, the *Wall Street Journal* interpreted the changes in selling as the beginning of a real bear market. Most experts counted on the Dow-Jones figures for an interpretation of what was happening on the market. Charles H. Dow had organized his financial service in 1882. At first he had published a short financial newsletter; by 1899 it had grown into the respected *Wall Street Journal*. The Dow-Jones Company had also developed a system of stock market averages in 1884, which had become an important tool of stock analysis by the 1920's. The averages were originally obtained by listing the eleven most active stocks representing indicators of trends in the stock market. Railroad stocks, commonly referred to as rails, were compiled first, but a separate average for industrial stocks was added in 1896. By January of 1929, an average for utilities and a combined average of all stocks were also computed. *The New York Times* also started producing its own averages in the 1920's.

For many years professional financial operators had studied the averages to make their decisions on stock dealings. These operators worked to maneuver and manipulate in carefully hidden ways. Moving in and out of the stock market, they would organize pools and syndicate operations to capitalize upon prices as they rose or fell. They made great profits, especially during the late twenties, while amateur speculators, also eager to make money, responded to the operators' maneuverings and bought stock that these men manipulated.

Speculators like Arthur Cutten, William C. Durant, Jesse Livermore, the Fisher brothers, the Van Sweringen brothers, and Michael J. Meehan had made and lost many fortunes. From the mid-twenties until the panic in 1929 these men moved in and out of the rising bull market, manipulating prices by clever pool operations.

William Crapo Durant had started the Buick Company and organized General Motors before he was removed as head of GM in 1920. From 1924 through the spring of 1929, as head of a syndicate of over twenty powerful millionaires, he manipulated some $4 billion in stocks.

Arthur Cutten had made $10 million on the wheat market by 1925. Then he turned to Wall Street and joined the Durant and Fisher brothers syndicate to try to make another fortune.

The seven Fisher brothers, children of a blacksmith, created the Fisher Body Company in 1908. This successful company was later bought by General Motors for about $200 million and the brothers joined forces with the Durant group to manipulate the bull market.

The two Van Sweringen brothers, Oris Paxton and Mantis James, were railroad-empire builders of the 1920's. In 1916 they had bought a

William C. Durant, powerful syndicate head of a group of millionaires who ruthlessly manipulated stocks. (Brown Brothers)

rundown railroad from the New York Central, called the Nickel Plate. From this beginning they built a pyramid of companies worth approximately $120 million before the panic.

Jesse Livermore, unlike these speculators on the bull market, was known as the King of the Bears, because he preferred to operate as the market moved down. Livermore began trading on the stock market as a young boy and went on to a spectacular lifetime of making and losing fortunes. He, too, joined the Durant group in the mid-twenties. In the fall of 1929 he made millions as a bear operator, selling short in great quantities of stock as prices declined.

To organize a pool, a number of traders would combine their resources to push up prices of a certain stock. They would choose one manager to take charge of manipulating the stock. The group then would buy the stock until interest was aroused and speculators would catch on that this security was an attractive bargain. Thus, buying would begin and prices would start to rise. More people would step in, happy to ride along with the wave and make a small share as the big manipulators made their profits. When the stock reached a peak of buying, the pool would quickly sell out and divide the proceeds with the syndicate they had organized. Then the price of the stock would fall back to its normal level as interest tapered off.

Speculators used various techniques to manipulate stocks. One was the "washed sale," illegal but practiced during the 1920's. A speculator would sell large numbers of shares to a second party, who would sell them to a third, and he in turn would sell them to a fourth prearranged buyer. This action would falsely indicate an active demand for the stock and its price would rise.

There was an old saying on the market which explained another technique — the "short sale":

> He who sells what isn't his'n,
> Must buy it back or go to pris'n.

In the "short sale," a group would negotiate a loan to borrow a large block of shares. These would be sold at a high price, calculating that the price was about to fall. When prices fell, the stock would be repurchased at its low price. The block of stock would be returned to the original lender, but the manipulator would keep the difference between the low price and the high price. Clever manipulators could make huge profits by "selling short," but it was disastrous to miscalculate and "sell short" when prices were rising.

"Radio" was one stock which showed just how speculators could make their fortunes by clever manipulations. It was the most glamorous speculative stock of the bull market. Like the automobile, the radio had become a great craze of the American people during the 1920's. In 1921, a few farsighted engineers had developed experimental radio stations. By 1923, stations were being established throughout the country. By the mid-twenties many homes had radios or crystal sets with

[21]

earphones to listen, for example, to the distinctive croon of Rudy Vallee and the rasping voices of Amos and Andy.

Radio Corporation of America (or Radio as it was called) was a leading producer of radio receivers. Its stock had been sold on the New York exchange since 1924. The price of the stock had remained at a steady level of between 40 and 50 points until it was discovered by one of the professional pool organizers. Michael Meehan took notice of radio's popularity and he formed a Radio pool of 63 members to push its price up. Soon amateur speculators saw its price climbing and Radio became the sudden rage of the market. People bought eagerly as its price rose. For a time, as many as 500,000 shares a day were traded, and in one four-day period in March, 1928, radio stock jumped 61 points. It rose from 85 ½ to 420 in 1928 and continued up to a high of 549 in mid-1929. Later the stock was split to adjust its price to a better selling level. When Meehan and his pool decided it was time to dissolve the operation, they had accumulated a $13-million investment. In the last two days of Radio's pool operation almost a million shares of stock were traded. Then the pool quickly sold its stock and made a $5-million profit long before Radio crashed in the panic.

One of the most audacious manipulators during the 1920's was Ivar Kreuger. Known as the International Match King, he came to the United States from Sweden in 1922 and eventually sold $148.5 million in securities to willing speculators. Kreuger once said, "Whatever success I have had may perhaps be attributable to three things; one is silence. The second is more silence, while the third is more silence." Kreuger operated silently to build up a worldwide complex of pyramiding companies and was respected in financial capitals of the world.

For years these professional manipulators had ridden along the crest of the bull market with their profitable pool and syndicate operations. Some of them had already taken their current profits out before

[22]

Ivar Kreuger, known as the Swedish "International Match King," because of his monopoly in the match manufacturing field. (Brown Brothers)

Wednesday, October 23, but others would soon be involved in driving down the market by selling short to make gains as the market fell. Yet on Wednesday morning when readers picked up early copies of *The New York Times* there was no indication that some pools would be forced to sell out that very day. In fact, the financial news dispelled some of the rising concern, for the paper predicted that bankers were willing to lend their support to the faltering stock market. It also reported rumors that the Federal Reserve Board would step in and lower rediscount rates to make borrowing easier. However, the Federal Reserve Board did not take this action on Wednesday.

Trading on the exchange floor opened uneventfully on Wednesday. However, during the morning a sudden break caused prices to skid. Selling increased. As prices continued to fall during the afternoon, losses became widespread. Then suddenly, in the final hour of the day, a flood of sales poured in. In one hour 2.6 million shares were traded and there was no final price rally. This was the first real major crash in the market. And it was also one of the quickest.

The strain of this unexpected selling showed on the stock ticker. It ran 104 minutes late after the market had closed at 3:00 P.M. and finally registered a new low point in the week-long price decline. During the last hour's sales, averages on fifty leading industrial stocks had fallen over eighteen points. This marked the largest decline since 1911. Paper losses of over $4 billion were recorded for the day. Many small speculators were wiped out.

Now there could be no uncertainty about the trend. It was plunging down. A bear market had overtaken the bull. Margin calls poured out of brokers' offices that night, but many unfortunate investors had no more money. They were frantic, knowing that their stock would be sold the next day for whatever price it could command. Other speculators reacted nervously to brokers' letters which urged them to wait until the market settled down before investing again. Even the boldest manipulators felt apprehensive.

Meanwhile, on the ocean liner *Berengaria*, as on other transatlantic ships, passengers were buying stock in the ship's brokerage office when news of the break started coming through. Abruptly, the party-like atmosphere changed as people squeezed into the room to watch the board boy list rapidly dropping prices. People skipped meals and took up a "deathwatch" as the hours progressed. All in all, 20,000 shares were traded from the *Berengaria* that day alone.

A spasm of uncertainty gripped brokers who gathered in hotels and speakeasies to talk of what would happen and to pass along current rumors. Word had spread that stock exchanges were going to close, that banks and brokerage houses were failing, and even that people were committing suicide by jumping from tall buildings in New York. Though the rumors were exaggerated, they led to heightened tension. That night Wall Street was disrupted by hundreds of messenger boys running through the financial district after being let off from work. Tossing torn ticker tape, they yelled and whooped as they ran through the streets. After several false riot reports were called in, police came and sent the boys home.

Brokers began to speak openly of tomorrow's bringing an even greater crash. They were gravely concerned over the day's selling which had swept many clients into insolvency. Few of them could actually conceive of the extent of disaster destined to descend within the next twenty-four hours. Nor could they predict that dawn would bring a day infamous in stock market history, a day that would forever be called Black Thursday. The volume of sales that day was 6,374,960. A look at the stock tables for Wednesday shows just how heavy losses were during the trading:

	HIGH	LOW	LAST	NET CHANGE
Allied Chemical	304	286	286⅛	−16⅛
American & Foreign Power	136¼	109	112	−23½
American Telephone & Telegraph	289	262	272	−15
Auburn Auto	337	250	260	−77
General Electric	341	313	314	−20
International Telephone & Telegraph	122	110¾	110¾	− 9⅝
Montgomery Ward	92⅞	82½	83¼	− 9¼
Radio	81⅝	67½	68½	−11¾
U.S. Steel	214¼	201⅝	204	− 8⅛

Thursday, October 24

BROKERS IN UPROAR AS MARKET BOILS

1,000 Mill Madly on Floor of Exchange and Thunder of Voices Is Heard Outside.

WORST STOCK CRASH STEMMED BY BANKS; 12,894,650-SHARE DAY SWAMPS MARKET; LEADERS CONFER, FIND CONDITIONS SOUND

New York Times, October 25, 1929

Fear was thick in the air as the heavy doors of the stock exchange opened that fine fall morning of October 24. All available employees were at their posts to handle the rush of telephone calls and paper work they expected that day. When the visitors' gallery opened, throngs of curious onlookers and anxious speculators jammed in to watch what would happen on the floor. One man in the crowd of spectators was Winston Churchill.

Trading became heavy as soon as the market opened. Thousands of margin speculators had been forced the night before to tell their brokers to sell their stock. Prices fell immediately, but for the first half-hour orders to buy and sell were absorbed in an orderly manner. Then large blocks of stock placed on the market by pools began to pile up faster than they could be sold. As selling gained momentum and prices fell, stop-loss sales were ordered. These were brokers' orders to sell if a stock fell to a certain point below the current price. Brokers placed these orders to protect themselves on the securities of customers who had not answered their margin calls.

At 10:30 A.M. the stock ticker already registered fifteen minutes behind trading. By eleven thirty it was forty-eight minutes behind, and nobody could determine actual prices. Blocks of 15,000 shares of Sinclair Oil, 15,000 shares of Standard Brands, 20,000 shares of General Motors increased the burden of selling. By eleven o'clock, just one hour after the market opened, a real stampede to "sell at any price" thundered through the exchange. Brokers had received imperative instructions.

"Sell, sell at any price!"

"Get out!"

"Sell at the market!"

Prices continued to tumble, sliding down five or ten points between listings. Some stocks were falling in value so rapidly that no buyer appeared at any price. These "air pockets" where no buyer at all could be found for important stocks frightened brokers most of all. In panic they shouted orders to sell or waited anxiously for a buyer to appear. They knew that they had to sell stocks for a customer in order to salvage something. Excited page boys dashed around from post to post waving orders to brokers, and scraps of paper piled unnoticed on the floor. Orders went astray and got lost in the debris. The volume of business overwhelmed the exchange. The scene had turned into a bedlam of confused cries and ringing telephones.

In other cities crowds gathered at their brokers' branch offices. To their horror they found it impossible to determine the value of their stocks. Prices had fallen so precipitously and volume had increased so rapidly that stock tickers could not provide current information. Tension grew as stockholders realized that they were not receiving current prices on the ticker. Even more upsetting, the bond ticker, which showed selected prices every ten minutes direct from the floor of the New York exchange, indicated prices far lower than the Translux projector showed on the wall.

People jammed telephone lines and telegraph offices but there was no way to get through to New York brokers on the exchange floor. Records for Western Union were broken as cables poured in from all over the world. Rumors spread as bewildered men found themselves unable to read quotations accurately. It was the practice to list only the last digit of a stock quotation on the ticker. In normal times the numbers were easy to decipher, but this day, as prices dropped with such swiftness, it was impossible to tell whether Radio was 61, 51, or 41, for only the number 1 was posted. As the ticker read: R 6.5.3.2½.1, one could not tell the actual price of Radio stock. Again, it would list: X 9.8.5.1½, and anxious stockholders looked at the quotations in confusion, for they could not be sure whether U.S. Steel was selling at 229, 219, or 209.

Back at the New York exchange some brokers grimly continued trying to sell stocks. Others crowded into one corner of the floor where a clerk shouted out current figures direct from a bond ticker, for they themselves could not find out what was happening to prices. By noon chaos in the visitors' gallery had reached such proportions that officials

Anxious faces in the crowds outside the Exchange mirror the anxiety of "Black Thursday," October 24, 1929. (United Press International)

had to close the gallery. Then another rumor circulated outside that the entire stock exchange had closed.

The spectators leaving the gallery merged with the large crowd that had gathered outside the exchange. A workman had climbed onto the roof of a nearby building to make repairs. People believed he was going to commit suicide and waited for him to leap. Talk spread through the crowd that eleven speculators had committed suicide, that regional stock exchanges had locked their doors, and that military personnel were on their way to guard the New York exchange.

Although the crowd remained peaceful, the chief of police nevertheless ordered men to the scene to quell any possible disturbance. By the middle of the afternoon 400 policemen were on duty to keep order in the streets. Newsmen arrived to get on-the-spot stories. Movie cameramen hurried around for newsreel shots of the crowd. Photographers scrambled to take action photos of the scene. The worst moments of Black Thursday were permanently recorded for all America to see.

By noon it became clear that nationwide panic was possible. Immediate action was imperative if the financial structure of the country was not to be jeopardized by the sudden stock collapse. At lunchtime the crowd milling around Broad and Wall streets recognized four of the nation's most prominent bankers arriving at the doors of J. P. Morgan & Company just opposite the exchange. They were Charles E. Mitchell, chairman of the National City Bank; Albert H. Wiggin, chairman of the Chase National Bank; William C. Potter, president of the Guaranty Trust Company; and Seward Prosser, chairman of the Bankers Trust Company. They were joined by Thomas W. Lamont, senior partner representing J. P. Morgan.

These men of vast financial power were not apprehensive that their own banks would fail. They realized that for the moment this was a crisis of the stock market, and their purpose in meeting was to decide how to pool their resources in order to support the market. All of them agreed that panic had to be prevented, for they knew from past experience that if stocks closed that day at the dangerously low levels to which they had already fallen, the result would be catastrophic. Brokerage houses would fail. This in turn might lead to a run of depositors on their banks.

The great financial institutions of the nation had to protect themselves by stabilizing the stock market if they could, and these five bankers came armed with pledges of support. During the twenty-minute session they quickly agreed to purchase necessary stocks to steady prices. Statements differ on exactly how much money was pledged, but the figure ranged from between $20 million and $40 million promised by each bank that day. At the end of their short meeting, Thomas Lamont emerged to face a barrage of reporters. "There has been a little distress selling on the stock exchange," he said. But he insisted that margins were being maintained, and that the situation had come about from a "technical condition" rather than from any fundamental difficulty.

The bankers maintained that all was well. News of this organized banking support spread across the floor quickly, as the bankers had intended it would. At one thirty, Richard Whitney, president of the exchange and a floor broker himself for the House of Morgan, walked boldly onto the floor. He headed toward the number two post where U.S. Steel was traded. There he placed a bid at 205 for 10,000 shares of steel, although steel was actually selling at 193½. When he received 200 shares, he left an order for the remainder. Then he continued around the floor from post to post, placing orders for similar purchases of fifteen or twenty other "blue chip" stocks. Other brokers representing the bankers did the same. Jubilant telephone clerks immediately relayed the news back to their brokerage houses, and word spread that the bankers had moved in with a promise of price support to halt the crash.

Brokers reacted just as the bankers had planned. Immediately after Lamont's noontime statement, a steadying trend in prices set in. Soon after that, prices, especially of those stocks the bankers had picked to support, started to gain back some of their losses. The panic of Black Thursday seemed to have been contained. As if by magic the pall lifted, and many stocks began to reverse their decline. The bold action of Whitney and his bankers' consortium brought back some confidence, stabilized prices, and encouraged a stock rally. By the close of day, trading seemed to be going in an orderly manner.

Yet what was the end result of this day of pandemonium? *The New York Times* industrials recorded a fall of 12 points in averages for the day, and the Dow-Jones industrials fell only 6.3 points. The situation was really worse than it seemed, however, for many stocks that made up the averages had been supported by the bankers' consortium while many others which were not supported and not among the *Times* averages fell to their lowest prices — and these had not rallied.

Due to Whitney's support, steel, despite the fact that it had dropped 10½ points earlier that day, actually gained 2 points by day's end. Mongtomery Ward had fallen 33 points but had sprung back 24 points for a total loss of 9. Radio had fallen 24 points but had come back for a loss of only 10¼ points. But Auburn Auto had fallen 70 points and even with a climb back had still lost 25 points. Thus, final prices did not accurately reflect the full extent of the crash that day. Many speculators had been ruined before the bankers' action saved the day for other, luckier stockholders. A volume of 12,894,650 shares had been traded, the largest to that time in history and a figure far above the previous high of 8,246,700 set on March 26, 1929.

Long after the closing gong, fatigued brokers tried to bring order out of the chaos of figures and paper work. Exhaustion and nerves had caused errors which had to be tracked down. Thousands of orders

Richard Whitney, floor man for the House of Morgan, whose bold buying action and that of his consortium helped steady prices on Black Thursday. Several times President of the New York Stock Exchange, Whitney later stood trial on charges of violating the Exchange's code of business ethics. (Brown Brothers)

had to be recorded. Letters and calls had to be sent for more money for margin accounts. Once more, clerks worked through the night to catch up before another onslaught might begin. Some workers actually fell ill from overwork, and nurses remained on duty for emergencies. One employee later told of telegraph operators working for 30 to 35 hours without sleep. Weary girls at the adding machines and typewriters fainted at their desks. In one firm 34 girls collapsed from exhaustion. In another, 19 had to be sent home. Restaurants sent in food, and hotels set up beds in corridors to put up weary workers.

Across the country that night uncertainty about where some accounts stood mingled with the despair of many who knew they had lost most of their money that day. Thousands had seen their dreams of wealth dissolve. Some sat staring at the moving figures on the tape in brokers' offices, still unable to believe that their profits were gone. To these men and women it was no comfort to know that Wall

Street bankers had pooled resources to support the market at noon, when they themselves had lost everything in the morning.

These people could not fully comprehend why the terrible break in prices had happened. They did not understand that it was due to the speculative orgy that had engulfed the nation. This excess of speculation had enabled too many people to buy stocks on margin. When their credit was gone, they were forced to dump blocks of stock on a market ill-equipped to absorb the sudden great volume.

For the moment organized bankers' support had saved some fortunate speculators and had steadied the market. But, for many people, that day of panic brought financial ruin and the end of hope. Indeed, it deserved the epithet of Black Thursday. A look at the following stock table shows a sample of the losses suffered:

	HIGH	LOW	LAST	NET CHANGE
Allied Chemical	286	265	284	− 2½
American & Foreign Power	115	88	97⅛	−14½
American Telephone & Telegraph	274¾	245	269	− 3
Auburn Auto	260	190	235	−25
General Electric	319¾	283	308	− 6
International Telephone & Telegraph	113¾	79	106	− 4¾
Montgomery Ward	84	50	74	− 9¼
Radio	70⅞	44½	58¼	−10¼
U.S. Steel	207⅛	193⅛	206	+ 2

Friday, October 25

STOCKS GAIN AS MARKET IS STEADIED;
BANKERS PLEDGE CONTINUED SUPPORT;
HOOVER SAYS BUSINESS BASIS IS SOUND

New York Times, October 26, 1929

A disillusioned America read about the events on Wall Street the night of Black Thursday. Meanwhile, brokers and bankers were making efforts to restore the nation's shattered confidence. Thirty-five influential brokerage firms took action. Hoping to sell optimism with advertising, they placed ads in eighty-five newspapers on Friday, urging the public to buy stock *now* at good, cheap prices. With a planned campaign on radio, in the newspapers, and in quickly mailed brokers' letters, they said that the worst was over; *now* was the opportune moment to buy: "We believe," the ads said, "that present conditions are favorable for advantageous investment in standard American securities."

Public opinion was temporarily influenced. At the exchange on Friday, October 25, prices held steady, and there was no new stampede to sell. True, volume was heavy, with nearly six million shares traded, but this was less than half the amount changing hands during the panic the day before. Prices advanced in some stocks, which climbed a few points higher than Thursday's closing. This was a good sign, for it reinforced the bankers' statements that there was no reason for public nervousness, that Wall Street was back under control, and that conditions remained sound.

At the White House, President Hoover convened his cabinet for a special meeting to hear Secretary of the Treasury Andrew Mellon report on the financial situation. Afterward, reporters crowded around the President. Hoover spoke confidently, adding his statement of optimism to the bankers' message. "The fundamental business of the country, that is production and distribution of commodities, is on a sound and prosperous basis," he told the nation.

The public seemed to believe the President. People wanted to feel that the crisis was over and that the stock market was simply adjusting itself. In fact, many began to talk hopefully of regaining money lost during the past week; they even spoke gratefully of bankers saving Wall Street from disaster. Apparently many did not realize that those same bankers who had organized support during the crisis had also helped organize the advertisements which appeared so opportunely on Friday and Saturday. Apparently, too, the public was not aware that, even as the bankers' group had acted to promote public confidence, they were at the same time acting privately to protect themselves.

Little by little, the bankers' pool (for that was what it was in effect) was quietly selling back many of the stocks they had purchased on Black Thursday. They obviously had no intention of getting caught in the next wave of liquidation, should one occur. Needless to say, they did not make these sales public, for this would have undermined their own advice that *now* was the best time to buy stocks.

Newspaper headlines on Saturday echoed the new confidence. "Only Yawns Recall Big Day in Wall Street," declared *The New York*

On Friday, the day after Black Thursday, anxious investors waited for further news outside the Exchange. Note Paramount News sound truck in the foreground. (United Press International)

Times. Brokers had urged the stock exchange to suspend trading on Saturday. They needed time to complete the massive job of bringing records up to date. But the governors of the exchange hesitated, afraid that not to open the market to trading would frighten the public.

Accordingly, they opened the exchange for a short trading period Saturday morning, and prices slipped several points before closing for the weekend. Despite this, some people listened to and believed the words of the president of a large trust company: "There will be no repetition of the break of yesterday . . . I have no fear of another comparable decline." But others were pessimistic. Senator King of Utah said skeptically, "Gambling in stock has become a national disease. . . .

[37]

It was inevitable that the day of reckoning would come." He predicted further price declines and demanded an investigation of the Federal Reserve System. But Senator Edge of New Jersey did not see things that way: "Congress cannot pass laws to prevent people spending their money."

As Congress hesitated over federal action, the public seemed to grow more confident about a quick market recovery. On Saturday, 80,000 fans escaped to the Yale-Army football game. Some took an open-air ride in their new automobiles, munched popcorn at the local movie theater, or joined friends at a speakeasy. Others discussed the latest market news, passing along current information. One big investor had bought stocks worth $1 million to show his confidence. A leading bank in Cleveland had just placed an order for $2 million to buy stocks. Here, apparently, was positive evidence that the market was returning to normal. Even so, speculators who had received a final, imperative margin call that weekend were not reassured. The message was familiar: more money must cover stocks bought on margin. Unfortunately, many had no further funds and no choice but to sell.

Despite Wall Street's advertising campaign, the weekend gave rise to some further anxiety among nervous professional speculators. They wondered what would happen on Monday morning. Brokers' offices on Wall Street remained open on Sunday. The street hummed with unaccustomed activity as many brokers received orders to sell. Sightseeing buses jammed the financial district. Big black limousines that would ordinarily have been cruising through the countryside on Sunday lined Wall and Broad streets as owners visited their brokers.

The period of artificially manufactured optimism that weekend turned out to be the calm before another storm. Black Thursday had been a prelude to the main event — the big crash which would resound throughout the nation during the coming week. Prices of Friday's trading had reflected the spirit of cautious optimism that still prevailed through that weekend:

	HIGH	LOW	LAST	NET CHANGE
Allied Chemical	286	283	286	+ 2
American & Foreign Power	104½	99½	102	+ 4½
American Telephone & Telegraph	272¾	265	265¾	− 3¼
Auburn Auto	240	224	225	−10
General Electric	311	300	305½	− 2½
International Telephone & Telegraph	107⅞	103⅛	106½	+ ½
Montgomery Ward	77¾	71¾	75	+ 1
Radio	61¾	58	60¼	+ 2
U.S. Steel	207	203½	204½	− 1⅞

Monday, October 28

Stocks Decline Heavily, Erasing All Year's Gains; Buying Near, Say Banks

New York *Herald Tribune*, October 29, 1929

In the past, panics have often been precipitated by overspeculation. As early as 1720 in England a frenzy of land speculation in the South Pacific brought about the bursting of the so-called South Sea Bubble. During that same period in France, the "Mississippi Bubble" collapsed after speculators invested too heavily in risky land ventures in the New World.

In the United States, panics have also occurred at periodic intervals, and each wrought its measure of business ruin and financial insolvency. Major crises had occurred in 1873, 1903, and 1907. The Panic of 1873 was caused by overspeculation and too rapid expansion during the era of westward migration. This financial crisis brought ruin to fifty-seven stock exchange firms as well as to the notorious financier Jay Cooke. The Great Panic of 1907 had its origins, like the 1929 crash, in wild speculation in stock and overextension of credit. During that crisis the eminent financier J. P. Morgan personally stepped in with $25 million to deposit in Manhattan banks, organizing support for brokers to avert a crisis. Thus, precedents had been set for the crash of 1929. But, although the stock market fall was a repetition of past economic disaster, it would explode with an impact greater than any other financial panic that had preceded it.

As the stock exchange opened for trading on Monday, October 28, there was great uncertainty. Many had built up hopes that the market would return to normal, but others knew that large blocks of stock would be sold that morning, and they feared the results. Shortly after trading began, the banker-created optimism of the weekend proved unsuccessful. When the first quotations appeared, hopes for a quick recovery faded. U.S. Steel, which everyone watched as the bellwether of the market, was already down 1¼ points. ITT had dropped 3 points, GE was off 7¼ points, and other outstanding blue chip stocks suffered similar losses.

The big traders had only waited to see which way the wind would blow. Now they saw that prices were falling and they took action to sell. Some operators had already placed stop-loss orders just below Saturday's closing prices to keep from losing more money in a possible downward rush of prices. Other speculators made their critical decisions as soon as they saw the low prices at day's opening. "Sell at any price," they ordered brokers, and the full fury of the panic resumed. Selling gained momentum, causing new losses. In the first half hour, prices fell 5 to 10 points. U.S. Steel now fell below 200; this drop was considered critical because it forecast the flight downward of other blue chip stocks.

Wave after wave of selling nudged prices lower and lower, as amateur and professional speculators alike tried to escape the deluge. This time, unfortunately, the bankers did not step into the breach to offer support to prices as they had the week before. Today they acted only in dire emergency when an air pocket appeared — that is, when no buyer at all stepped in to bid on an issue. Only then did they plug up the air pocket by buying up the issue. Today the bankers were powerless to control the scare that was sweeping the country. They had only agreed to see to it that the market continued functioning. If disaster came, it would take place in an orderly manner.

The fall continued. As the ticker dropped farther behind, the confusion of past days reappeared in force. Gray-faced brokers yelled hoarsely around important posts on the floor. They sold stocks at any price they could get, selling out big and little speculators alike. Succumbing to the mass wave of fright, investors who had survived the initial blows now dumped their stocks. Even men owning stocks outright, with no margin demands facing them, were shaken by growing nervousness and they, too, sold at a loss. Big pools were cleaned out, and rich men were hard hit.

A slight rally appeared just after one o'clock, but then prices slid down again. They fell through their low point of the past Thursday, as big traders dumped 100,000-share blocks for whatever they would bring. A total of 9.2 million shares were traded Monday, but 3 million of those shares were sold during the final hour alone. This fact paralyzed brokers and speculators most of all, for there had been no rally during the final hour. This forecast even greater losses for the next day. Dow-Jones averages declined 38.33 points, almost 13 percent during that single day. Security values lost a total of $14 billion, which meant that many men were ruined.

Finally, on Monday afternoon at 4:30 P.M., the bankers' consortium again convened. But this time their discussion was not so optimistic. Afterward they told reporters that they had no intention of organizing buying support, that they could not maintain prices to protect anyone's profit. They could only hope to help maintain an orderly market. This was terrible news for tired brokers. As they struggled with paper work once more throughout the night, they knew that the bottom had not yet been reached. Although Auburn Auto had already fallen 165 points, Otis Elevator over 60 points, G.E. 47½ points, and other companies had absorbed similar losses, brokers were fearful that tomorrow would bring an even greater crisis.

The premonitions of disaster that haunted the weary men of Wall Street that night were well-founded, for the next day would prove to be the most devastating in all stock market history. A glance at what happened to prices on Monday shows the extent of losses suffered:

	HIGH	LOW	LAST	NET CHANGE
Allied Chemical	275	231	245	−36
American & Foreign Power	96½	72¼	77½	−21¾
American Telephone & Telegraph	263	232	232	−34
Auburn Auto	220	175	190	−25
General Electric	290¼	250	250	−47¼
International Telephone & Telegraph	100	85	88	−15
Montgomery Ward	72¼	58½	59½	−15⅜
Radio	58	39¾	40¼	−18⅜
U.S. Steel	202½	185	186	−17½

Tuesday, October 29

STOCKS COLLAPSE IN 16,410,030-SHARE DAY, BUT RALLY AT CLOSE CHEERS BROKERS; BANKERS OPTIMISTIC, TO CONTINUE AID

New York Times, October 30, 1929

During the early morning hours of Tuesday, October 29, 1929, rain started falling in New York City. It washed the dust off lower Manhattan, leaving Wall Street clean. Dawn broke to gray and drizzling skies that set an appropriately somber tone for the day. Gloom hung in the dismal morning air as stock exchange clerks and brokers came up from underground subways for another day's labor in the market.

From the moment the gong sounded the opening of trading, blocks of stock were placed for sale on the market at any price. As the first quotations appeared over the ticker, men looked in disbelief at the numbers. Prices were spiraling downward — with gaps of 5 or 10 points between drops. Some shares were falling as many as 42 points below yesterday's closing prices and continued descending as large parcels were offered for whatever they would bring.

It was clear that this day's events would be grim. Brokers rushed from post to post trying to sell stocks before their customers were

[44]

ruined. But the orders choked the lines of communications and thwarted attempts at orderly operation. In the first half hour alone, 3.3 million shares were traded. As the atmosphere grew steadily more confusing, brokers started screaming orders to sell in 50,000- and 100,000-share blocks of stock before the rapidly declining prices could bring ruin to many speculators and leave others deeply in debt to their brokers.

Today even formerly conservative stockholders, who up till now had kept aloof from the panic, themselves began to fall victim to the hysteria that was seizing the financial world. These men dumped large blocks of stock on the market, creating greater chaos than before and causing prices to drop even lower. By now a wild pandemonium of selling engulfed the entire exchange. The din of yelling brokers, ringing telephones, and shouting messenger boys expanded to a roar which could be heard outside the building.

As the morning wore on, ticker tapes started to fall behind once more. Eight million shares were sold in the first two hours alone. By midmorning, the consortium of bankers agreed to take action. They needed to take measures to prevent the stock panic from precipitating a general money panic in which banks would be imperiled by a run on cash. Accordingly, the Board of Governors, the forty men who established policy for the exchange, called for a private noon meeting. Knowing that their every move would be scrutinized, the governors stole down by twos and threes to a small room directly beneath the main trading floor. Some governors argued that the exchange should be closed immediately; others insisted that shutting it down would lead to even greater panic. At that time this body had complete freedom to make administrative decisions, yet at the grave noontime gathering that day they could not agree on action. Tension mounted and tempers flared. Finally, they postponed any decision until they could meet

[45]

On Black Tuesday, October 29, the bottom really fell out of the market, with leading stocks plummeting $40, $50, and even $60 a share. Here gloomy crowds gather outside the Exchange, as thousands of other investors rushed to pawn silver or jewelry to raise more "margin." (*Brown Brothers*)

again that evening. Thus they left the panic free to run its course to the end of the day.

After this meeting, the consortium of bankers met again. They wanted to make it clear that they would continue to support the market, although they only intended to do so during moments when air pockets appeared. Strongly denying rumors that they were selling huge blocks of stock, they did not reveal that they had already sold much stock the previous week.

For some time large corporations had been freely loaning money to brokers at high rates of interest, making great profits for the corporations. Now, in this moment of crisis, they decided to recall these loans. Some market speculation had been based upon the loans, which amounted to over two billion dollars made to large Wall Street brokerage firms. When these corporations called back the loans, the crisis intensified. The bankers' consortium now considered the possibility that the firms whose loans were recalled could become insolvent if they were not given immediate help. As a result, some bankers personally took responsibility. They reduced margin requirements for bank loans to brokers, lowering rates from 40 to 25 percent to save some brokers' houses from insolvency. In turn, these brokers' firms lowered their margin requirements to customers below the 25 percent margin some had required. This saved precarious accounts which would have fallen if more margin had been demanded.

Accordingly, grim-faced bankers authorized a billion dollars in loans to brokers' firms, even beyond their resources. It was an action that took fortitude, for bankers were assuming responsibility for loans worth millions of dollars, secured by collateral which might prove worthless by day's end. Historian Frederick Lewis Allen described one banking official who that day took over loan after loan for his bank. When one of his officers announced to him that the bank was insolvent,

[47]

the gray-faced banker replied, "I dare say," and continued without pause to authorize additional loans from the bank. By his bold action, he saved more than one company from ruin.

Brokers and employees tried their best to deal with the torrent of sales and transfers. One broker carefully stored up orders in a large wastepaper basket to work on when he had a free moment. Some issues of stock actually "vanished" completely that day. They were withdrawn from the market so that they could neither be bought nor sold. This avoided sacrificing the stock at disastrously low prices. The steady drop in values continued until the last fifteen minutes of the day. Then a brief respite brought a slight rally in prices.

When the stock exchange closed that afternoon, the most devastating day in stock market history was over. More than 16 million shares had been traded in the collapse, and billions of dollars in market values were wiped out. The Dow-Jones industrial averages fell 30.57 points, but many stocks had dropped below that mark before the final fifteen-minute rally (which brought them back slightly). At nightfall a stunned nation surveyed the wreckage. Some entire fortunes and life savings disappeared in the dramatic end of the mighty bull market. A number of rich men now found themselves bankrupt or deeply in debt. Some brokerage firms doubted whether they were still solvent. As wealthy travelers sailed home from Europe aboard fancy ocean liners, they crowded into wireless rooms to send frantic orders to their brokers to sell. But it was too late. Some would dock in New York to face a life of considerably less luxury.

That night the Board of Governors convened again to consider closing the exchange. But because the last-minute rally had brought prices of some major issues up somewhat, they felt they could keep it open the next day. Even as they met, Wall Street was in a state of physical and emotional collapse. But once more men toiled wearily through the night. Restaurants stayed open to feed them and hotels again saved beds for tired workers.

The great bull market of the Roaring Twenties had crashed. It only remained for workers to clean up the debris and straighten out confused records, while stricken speculators tried to calculate their losses. Following is a small sampling of the losses suffered on the market on Black Tuesday, October 29:

	HIGH	LOW	LAST	NET CHANGE
Allied Chemical	218	204¾	210	−35
American & Foreign Power	73	50	55	−27½
American Telephone & Telegraph	230	204	204	−28
Auburn Auto	175	120	130	−60
General Electric	245	210	222	−28
International Telephone & Telegraph	76	61	71	−17
Montgomery Ward	56	49½	53¾	− 5¾
Radio	40	26	38½	− 1¾
U.S. Steel	192	166½	174	−12

Monday, November 4

STOCKS SAG 2 TO 17 POINTS IN DAY OF ORDERLY SELLING; SESSIONS CUT TO 3 HOURS

New York Times, Tuesday, November 5

The men of Wall Street who had shuffled papers all through the night of Black Tuesday started work the next morning exhausted and uncertain. They could no longer predict what would happen in their world. But to their relief, Wednesday, October 30, brought a revival of their spirits. Instead of continuing the disastrous decline of the previous day, prices actually started to level off.

At this point, the president of the exchange, Richard Whitney, felt it safe to announce the board's decision to close the exchange. It would remain open only briefly for trading on the following day, Thursday, he said, and then it would cease trading for the remainder of the week. Hoarse cheers echoed through the exchange hall at Whitney's announcement, for brokers needed rest and recuperation from the unrelenting nervous strain and work load of the past week.

On Wednesday there was good news. U.S. Steel unexpectedly declared an extra dividend. American Can Company did the same. These were acts by big business calculated to bring increased public confidence that the worst of the crash had passed. Even the venerable John D. Rockefeller joined other influential financiers who tried to erase public fear. He made an optimistic statement stressing solid business conditions: "My son and I have for some days been purchasing sound common stocks."

Even so, recovery was actually not in sight. In fact, prices had not yet reached their lowest point on Black Tuesday, October 29. They would continue to slide lower and lower, until two weeks later in November, they would finally hit bottom. They would continue to drop in 1930, 1931, and 1932. But on the present Wednesday and Thursday many still hoped for recovery. They watched on Wednesday as the market rallied and industrials regained 31 points. Several times on those two days relieved brokers who gathered around ticker tapes broke into loud cheers when they read rising quotations.

When trading was suspended for the week after Thursday's short session, an air of hope had replaced the gloom of Black Tuesday. Some people felt that the market had already begun to stabilize. They pointed to the good news that seemed to back up their opinion. The Federal Reserve Board of New York finally reduced the discount rate from 6 to 5 percent. This, they believed, would encourage greater lending. Others were convinced by the recent gains that the market had already begun to bounce back. Rising prices reassured some speculators that when trading resumed the next Monday, November 4, they would be wise to move in quickly to take advantage of low prices. That weekend they sent orders to their brokers to buy stocks before a bull market set in and prices rose again.

Amateur speculators, the men who had taken such a severe beating shortly before, seemed to be eternal optimists. They would not give up. Following the trail of the professional speculators and believing thereby that they could make easy money, some of these small-time

[51]

speculators withdrew what was left of their life savings to buy one or two shares of a stock. Others pawned jewelry, borrowed on their life insurance, or sought a few dollars from finance companies to try a last desperate attempt to recoup lost profits. Even the New York *Herald Tribune* echoed the surprising return of optimism. Monday morning, November 4, headlines read: "WALL ST. EXPECTS RECORD REVIVAL OF BULL MARKET TODAY."

But even as the papers hit the street on Monday, the rosy predictions proved wrong. Prices did not rise. They opened sharply off that morning, skidded down, and did not stop. The better the stock, it seemed, the lower its value fell in a steady plunge that continued through the first week in November. Now new despair descended on speculators. Thousands had lost everything on this last gamble to make money. The full impact of the market collapse sank in for the first time. There would be no more foolhardy talk of a sudden revival of the great bull market. The bull market was dead.

Yet many people who had been waiting for a fortune to fall in their laps did not blame their own overspeculative behavior for the present state of affairs. Rather, they sought all sorts of scapegoats. Some claimed that Divine Providence was scourging them for their greed. Some blamed the bankers or the Federal Reserve Board, while others pointed to a "foreign plot." A few even turned to astrology and blamed the planets for the calamity.

While financiers tried to encourage hope, they could not by cheerful talk halt this latest decline. John D. Rockefeller, who rarely spoke publicly, made another attempt to reassure the demoralized nation. He announced that he had put in a bid to buy a million shares of his own company, Standard Oil of New Jersey. To which comedian Eddie Cantor replied, "Sure, who else has any money left?" Julius

Rosenwald, a noted philanthropist and board chairman of Sears, Roebuck, said that his company would guarantee margin accounts of its employees. Public utilities tycoon Samuel Insull did the same. Dr. Julius Klein, Assistant Secretary of Commerce, said in a radio speech that business was sound and that only four percent of the nation's families were affected by the crash.

Many had lost, but a few were destined to gain. During that week Ford Motor Company placed advertisements in the nation's newspapers to announce price cuts in automobiles. All popular models would henceforth sell for $14 to $200 less. And the State of New York announced that it had earned almost $5 million in taxes on stock transactions. Still, none of these actions seemed able to stem the downward plunge of stock values. The descent continued despite reassuring speeches, despite action by the Federal Reserve Board to further lower the discount rate from 5 to 4½ percent, despite U.S. Steel's decision to issue a special dividend, and despite news that the exchange would investigate people engaged in "selling short."

At this point, the crash began to take its toll in human and individual tragedy, as long-rumored suicides turned into fact. In New York City the president of a trust firm took his life; two wholesale produce merchants jumped to their deaths in the city; and J. J. Riordan, a prominent Democrat and bank president, shot himself. In Philadelphia, two brokers shot themselves. In Chicago a grain broker killed himself with gas, and in Rochester the president of the gas and electric company took his life.

During the week Wall Street was further demoralized by false rumors. Some said that the exchange would close permanently. Others gossiped that bear pools were flooding the market with these very rumors, or that villainous bear operators had caused the crash by their manipulation of prices. Most depressing, however, was the continuing price slump. On November 4, trading figures showed how prices had dropped again after the temporary recovery of October 30:

	HIGH	LOW	LAST	NET CHANGE
Allied Chemical	244	231	235	−16
American & Foreign Power	86¼	79	79	−12⅝
American Telephone & Telegraph	248¼	233	237	− 9¾
Auburn Auto	215	201	201	− 9
General Electric	249	234	235	−17
International Telephone & Telegraph	93¾	85½	86¼	− 8¾
Montgomery Ward	72	68⅛	68⅝	− 4⅝
Radio	48	42	43¾	− 6¼
U.S. Steel	142¾	143	142	+ 2

Wednesday, November 13

Further Bad Breaks

*Severe Pressure Forces Leaders to
New Lows—Bears Active*

Wall Street Journal, Wednesday, November 13

Further bad breaks in the stock market continued beyond November 4. The bears were active, as they would be for the next two and a half years. A look at the daily changes in the Dow-Jones industrial averages tells the story:

Monday, November 4–down 15.83 points
Tuesday, November 5–closed, Election Day
Wednesday, November 6–down 25 points
Thursday, November 7–up 6.06 points
Friday, November 8–down 1.66 points
Monday, November 11–down 16.14 points
Tuesday, November 12–down 10.65 points

Wednesday, November 13, could be said officially to mark the end of an era. On that day the lowest point in the crash was reached. The unrestrained optimism of the New Age of Business was replaced with sober pessimism. The Jazz Age was at an end.

Trading on the market on November 13 resumed in a normal fashion. Prices kept dribbling downward. A feeling of gloom began to set in. Indeed, most brokers and speculators had begun to take the downward prices as a matter of course. Some relieved the tension by

The caption on this contemporary cartoon from Life *read: "Up three points? My gawd, I jumped too soon!"*

passing along humorous anecdotes that were beginning to make the rounds. One story told that hotel clerks in New York City were asking each new guest whether he was taking a room for sleeping or for jumping. Another told of two men jumping together; they had a joint account.

An issue of the old *Life* magazine (which itself went out of business shortly thereafter) had a cartoon showing two hoboes riding in a boxcar. One hobo said to the other: "It seems like only yesterday that I had stock in this company." Another story circulated around New York about suicide in the East River. It was said that each morning a fleet of top hats could be seen floating past Manhattan — minus their owners.

But these stories only relieved the fear momentarily. They did not delay the relentless downward spiral of stock prices. By the end of the day on November 13, the market average had again dropped seriously. This time it was down 11.05 points.

In the space of two months, from September 3 to November 13, 1929, the stock market had gone from its highest to its lowest mark of the year. The value of the average share had been cut just about in half by the great crash. For the remaining weeks of 1929, the market steadied, but then it continued to fall in a steady progression for the next two and a half years.

Aftermath of the Great Crash

The economic factors that had triggered the great crash now set off a general malaise throughout the land. The great depression had started. Buoyed by heavy public investment in the company's stock, large factories had been geared to full production for the age of prosperity. Now that stock was almost worthless. Frightened consumers were no longer splurging on every new gadget. Production on the assembly lines had to be severely reduced, and the factories had no alternative but to lay off many workers.

This assembly-line slowdown brought with it a multiplying effect. When an auto factory in Detroit laid off a thousand workers, it meant fewer orders for steel from Pittsburgh. The steel mills in turn had to lay off workers. This meant less money for clothes and food, so soon department stores and groceries were laying off clerks. These people in turn had less money for cars, so auto companies reduced production and laid off another thousand employees. As unemployment rose, men went out in the streets in search of jobs and food for their families. Soup kitchens were set up, and hungry, haggard men formed long lines for a cup of broth and a piece of bread. Some enterprising men bought bushels of apples and stood on street corners to resell them for a nickel apiece.

Banks were among the institutions hit hardest by the crash and the depression. Many banks had engaged in the questionable practice of using their customers' savings to gamble on speculative investments on the stock market. When the market fell, not only did the banks lose their gamble; their customers lost their life's savings. Between 1929 and 1932, more than 5,000 banks failed in the United States.

[58]

Gradually, poverty and despair spread throughout the land. Loan companies insisted on payments and foreclosed when the money was not forthcoming. People lost their vacuum cleaners, then their refrigerators, their radios, their Model A Fords, and eventually even their houses. In the Midwest, farms fell idle, and great stretches of plains, freshly plowed to sow the wheat of prosperity, were abandoned to the wind. Storms blew the land into great dust bowls of desolation. The poor and the unemployed who lost their homes and farms moved into shanties on the outskirts of cities. They huddled their families together in flimsy cardboard and tar-paper shacks. Many migrated west to seek work in the more prosperous farms and fruit orchards of California. But even there they were forced to find housing in shantytowns, called "Hoovervilles" after the man who was President during these terrible years.

From the 1929 crash onward, President Hoover continued to try to reassure the nation. "Business and industry have turned the corner," he said on January 21, 1930, two months after the crash. But around the corner even worse conditions prevailed. "We have now passed the worst," he declared on May 1, 1930. His secretary of labor, James J. Davis, concurred. "Courage and resourcefulness are already swinging us back to the road of recovery," Davis said on July 28, 1930. But the worst along that road was not yet in sight.

By December, 1930, when the situation had not improved, Hoover sought to restore some hope by telling Congress that "The fundamental strength of the nation's economy is unimpaired." It did little good.

The stock market crash of 1929 slowly began to take its toll among the professional speculators, those men who had done so much to manipulate the market into its precarious position. Jesse Livermore and William Durant, pool organizers who had made millions in the

Poverty, despair, and hunger came to the nation following the crash. Scenes such as these — breadlines and apple-sellers in New York — were typical of depression years. (Brown Brothers)

1920's, were reduced to abject poverty. Mike Meehan, the man who promoted radio stock to its all-time high, ended his years penniless in the thirties. That master manipulator, Ivar Kreuger, the so-called Swedish Match King, was driven to ruin. His stock, which sold at $120 a share at its peak in 1929, fell to 50 cents a share by 1932. Later, a congressional investigation revealed that he had forged bonds and swindled investors out of millions. In March, 1932, the Match King died by committing suicide in a Paris hotel.

Finally, on a hot day in July, 1932, the market hit its lowest point. Only 700,000 shares were traded that July 8, a poor showing compared with the millions on a typical day in 1929. The Dow-Jones industrial averages had dropped 89 percent below the level of Black Tuesday, October 29, 1929. *The New York Times* averages showed the market at 58 on July 8, 1932, compared to 224 on November 13, 1929. Quotations of typical stocks tell the dramatic story of the great stock market debacle in stark figures:

	HIGH DAY Sept. 3, 1929	LOW DAY Nov. 13, 1929	FINAL LOW July 8, 1932	NET CHANGE
Allied Chemical	354	198	45½	−308½
American & Foreign Power	160⅛	51	2½	−157⅝
American Telephone & Telegraph	302½	207	72⅛	−230⅜
Auburn Auto	497	130¼	44⅞	−452⅛
General Electric	391	173	9⅜	−381⅝
International Telephone & Telegraph	147½	53½	3⅞	−143⅝
Montgomery Ward	134½	49⅞	4⅜	−130⅛
Radio	98½	28¾	3⅝	− 94⅞
U.S. Steel	257⅝	151½	21½	−236⅛

Epilogue: The Lesson Learned

The story of the stock crash did not really end in abject tragedy, for the nation learned a lesson from the experience and ultimately gained better market safeguards and procedures. Even before the bottom was hit on July 8, 1932, the Hoover administration began a congressional investigation of Wall Street practices. In April, 1932, the Senate Committee on Banking and Currency started conducting hearings that lasted for two years and produced 12,000 pages of testimony.

When President Franklin D. Roosevelt came into office in 1933, he set about in his first one hundred days to propose sweeping new legislation to help cure the ills of the nation. Roosevelt dramatically closed all the banks until economic order could be restored. He brought swift enactment of the Glass-Steagall Banking Act which made banks divorce savings departments from investment activities in order to protect the savers' dollars from speculative gambling.

Further important legislation came out of the Senate's investigations. First was the Securities Act of 1933. This brought new control over the stock market. Then came the Securities and Exchange Act of 1934, which established the Securities and Exchange Commission to regulate Wall Street.

These acts limited the amount of credit and the sources of credit for speculative stock dealing. They also established strict requirements for purchasing stock on margin. They outlawed pool operations and "wash" sales. They required full disclosure of all information about stocks and bonds. They placed strict limits on the amount of speculation by insiders in the stocks and bonds of their own companies. In the years since the enactment of these laws, the stock market has made a complete recovery and steady progress toward the most prosperous era of all time.

In the minds of many, the great stock market crash of 1929 will always be a reminder. Unregulated manipulation, unrestrained optimism, and undisciplined hedonism caused an economic crash that reverberated around the world. Its repercussions were felt for years of economic stagnation and depression. A more sober, puritanical, and watchful nation had to rebuild its financial institutions. Hopefully, the proper lessons have been learned and such a financial disaster will never happen again.

Selected Bibliography

Allen, Frederick Lewis. *Only Yesterday*. New York: Harper & Row, 1931.

De Bedts, Ralph. *The New Deals S.E.C.: The Formative Years*. New York: Columbia University Press, 1964.

Faulkner, Harold Underwood. *American Economic History*. New York: Harper & Brothers, 1960.

Galbraith, John Kenneth. *The Great Crash, 1929*. Boston: Houghton Mifflin Company, 1954.

Lefevre, Edwin. *Reminiscences of a Stock Operator*. Larchmont, New York: American Research Council, 1964.

Leffler, George L. *The Stock Market*. New York: The Ronald Press Co., 1963.

Leuchtenberg, William E. *The Perils of Prosperity, 1914-1932*. Chicago: University of Chicago Press, 1958.

Mayer, Martin. *Wall Street: Men & Money*. rev. ed. New York: Harper & Brothers, 1959.

Noyes, Alexander Dana. *The Market Place: Reminiscences of a Financial Editor*. Boston: Little Brown, 1938.

Patterson, Robert T. *The Great Boom and Panic 1921-1929*. Chicago: Henry Regnery Co., 1965.

Prosperity Decade: From War to Depression: 1917-1929. The Economic History of the United States, Vol. VIII, New York: Rinehart & Company, Inc., 1947.

Sobel, Robert. *The Big Board: A History of the New York Stock Market*. New York: The Free Press, 1965.

Sparling, Earl. *Mystery Men of Wall Street*. New York: Greenberg Publishers, 1930.

Thomas, Dana L. *The Plungers & the Peacocks*. New York: G. P. Putnam's Sons, 1967.

Tyler, Poyntz, ed. *Securities, Exchanges and the SEC*. The Reference Shelf, Vol. 37, No. 3. New York: H. W. Wilson Co., 1965.

Wector, Dixon. *The Age of the Great Depression 1929-1941*. New York: The Macmillan Company, 1948.

Index